Claire Steel

C000205294

Scottish
Baby Names

Betty Kirkpatrick

Crombie Jardine
PUBLISHING LIMITED
Office 2
3 Edgar Buildings
George Street
Bath
BA1 2FJ

www.crombiejardine.com
www.twitter.com/crombiejardine

First published in 2010
by Crombie Jardine Publishing Limited

Copyright © Crombie Jardine Publishing, 2010

ISBN 978-1-906051-25-9

Written by Betty Kirkpatrick

Printed and bound in China

Contents

INTRODUCTION

Scottish Baby Names covers not only those names which are Scottish in origin, but those names which are, or have been, particularly common in Scotland.

Over the centuries names in Scotland have been much influenced by immigrants, from the Vikings in the north, to the Norman French who came into Scotland from England after the Norman Conquest, and the Irish who came to Scotland, especially during the mid-nineteenth century as a result of the potato famine. This influence is reflected in *Scottish Baby Names*, but the book does not cover ethnic names which have become known in Scotland as a result of relatively recent immigration. Such names do not, as yet, occur in numbers which are statistically significant enough to appear in lists of most frequent or most popular names.

Given that this is a relatively small book, it cannot, obviously, be comprehensive in its coverage of names, but it gives a valuable insight into the naming process in Scotland, both ancient and modern.

The Scots method of naming children has changed greatly in recent years. Traditionally Scots children were named after other family members. For example, many families followed the custom of naming the eldest two sons and daughters after the four grandparents, usually the eldest son and eldest daughter being named after the paternal grandfather and grandmother and the next eldest son and daughter being named after the maternal grandfather and grandmother. Other children, of which there were likely to be far more in number than in the average modern family, were frequently named after their parents, aunts, uncles and close family friends.

Usually there was little sign of variety and each generation was likely to have much the same range of traditional names. These came from different sources. Some of them, such as Angus, Torquil, Fergus, Mhairi and Catriona, were Gaelic in origin and were originally particularly popular among Highland families. Other names were popularized by Scottish kings and queens, such as Robert, Malcolm, Margaret, Alexander and Charles. Some names were biblical in origin, including John, James, Mary and Elizabeth.

In recent years there has been a distinct change in the habits of Scottish parents when it comes to naming their children. Few families adhere to the system of naming offspring after family members any more and if they did, few would get further than the grandparents' names, families generally being much smaller than in the past.

Nowadays, parents spend a long time poring over books to choose names that they particularly like. Sometimes they decide to be particularly innovative and make up names.

Modern names which have become popular, perhaps because of a celebrity with the name, include Brooke, Kayleigh, Kylie and Paige. Side by side with this trend goes an increase in the use of Celtic names, both Scottish and Irish, such as Caitlin, Callum, Connor, Kieran, Liam, Mairi/Mhairi, Niamh, Nuala and Sean. Some Welsh names have also become popular in Scotland recently, including Megan, Owen and Rhys, often now spelt Reece.

Also a feature of recent trends in naming children is the resurgence in popularity of names which were once popular, although not necessarily particularly popular in Scotland, but which had gone out of fashion. Many of these are girls' names, including Charlotte, Emma, Emily and Lucy. There has also been an increase in popularity of Old Testament names such as Daniel, Joshua, Nathan, Rachel, Rebecca, Hannah and Leah.

Many traditional first names have diminutive or pet forms. In recent times many of these, such as Archie,

INTRODUCTION

Ben, Ellie, Jamie, Katie, Sam and Vicky/Vikki have become first names in their own right, many overtaking the parent name in popularity.

There has been a tradition in Scotland, more so than in other countries, of using surnames as first names, particularly male first names. To some extent this tradition has continued into modern times and, for example, Cameron appears in the top ten in recent lists of most popular boys' names in Scotland, recently also being used occasionally as a female first name.

Many of the first names in this book have been selected because they featured recently in the top fifty most popular names in Scotland, the information being obtained from the General Register Office for Scotland via the Internet. Other names featured include traditional or older names which have once been popular, although they may no longer be. Who knows? They may return to popularity one day since the choice of first names is subject to relatively swift changes in fashion.

Apologies if your name or that of your child is not here. There are so many first names that it was not possible to include all of them with the space available in the book.

Scottish Baby Names is a valuable source of information for Scots in Scotland, for the many people of Scots heritage who live elsewhere but are interested in their roots, and for people who are just interested in things Scottish. Moreover, its handy size makes it an ideal book for browsing through.

Betty Kirkpatrick, 2010

GIRLS' NAMES

Abbie

Abbie is a diminutive form of **Abigail**, although it is now often used as a female first name in its own right. It has become very popular in Scotland.

Abigail

The name is Hebrew in origin, and means 'father rejoiced'. Abigail was the wife of Nabal in the Bible, but married David after Nabal's death. The name was recorded in Scotland in the early seventeenth century, but only relatively recently achieved popularity. **Gail** is a short form of Abigail which became popular from around the middle of the twentieth century.

See **Abbie**.

Agnes

Agnes is not a Scottish name by derivation. It comes from a Greek word meaning 'chaste' and St Agnes was the name of a third-century virgin martyr who was sanctified. The name Agnes was widespread in several countries for centuries and was particularly popular in Scotland for a long time, only going into decline in the second part of the twentieth century. Sometimes shortened to **Aggie** or **Aggy** or to **Nessa** or **Nessie**, Agnes is occasionally reversed in spelling to form the name Senga, although this is nowadays even less common than it was formerly. Unlike Agnes, Senga seems to have been restricted to Scotland. In Scotland people christened Agnes were sometimes called Nancy, although this is also a diminutive form of Anne and a first name in its own right.

Aileen

Aileen is a form of **Eileen** which is particularly popular in Scotland. Both forms of the name are Irish in origin, derived from *ail* meaning 'noble'.

Ailish

Ailish is the Gaelic equivalent of **Alice**, which was originally a Norman French name. It has long been popular in Ireland, but has recently also become popular in Scotland with the increase in interest in Celtic names.

Ailsa

Ailsa has been used in Scotland for more than a century and there has been some dispute about its origin. Some writers have suggested that it is a peculiarly Scottish form of the name **Elsa**, while another suggestion links it with Ealasaid, the Gaelic form of **Elizabeth**. However, most commentators tend to derive the name from the Scottish place name Ailsa Craig, a rocky island in the Clyde estuary, off the coast of Ayrshire.

Aimee

see **Amy**

Alice, Alison

Alice is derived from a French version of the German name Adelheid meaning 'nobility'. The name is recorded in Scotland in the twelfth century. In Scotland **Alison** was once used as a diminutive form of Alice, but it is now a common name in its own right.

Amber

This name is derived from the yellowish-brown fossil and jewel called amber. The word is Arabic in origin. The name appears in the top fifty in recent lists of most popular girls' names in Scotland.

Amy

Amy is derived from the feminine form of the past participle of the French verb *amer*, the modern form of which is *aimer*, 'to love'. The alternative spelling **Aimee** is nearer the original French form. Amy has recently become very popular, finding a place in the top ten girls' names in Scotland for 2009.

Ann, Anne, Anna, Annie

Ann, with its alternative spelling **Anne**, is derived from the Hebrew name **Hannah** meaning 'favoured one'. The name has enjoyed the same long-term popularity in Scotland as it has in other English-speaking countries. One difference is that the form **Annie** was, until fairly recently, particularly popular in Scotland. Anna is also a popular form of the name in Scotland.

Annabel, Annabella

Annabel does not sound especially Scottish, but its associations with Scotland go back as far as the twelfth century. Its popularity historically may have had something to do with its royal connections, because the mother of James I was Annabel Drummond (1394-1437). In origin it is likely to be a form of the name Amable, itself derived from the Latin word *amabilis*, meaning 'lovable'. Amable developed into the name Mable.

Antonia

see **Antony, Anthony** *in* **Boys' Names**

Aoife

Aoife is a Celtic female first name which is pronounced *ee-fa*. The name, which means 'radiant', 'joyful', has been popular in Ireland for a long time. According to Irish legend, Aoife was a great female warrior. The name has recently become popular in Scotland, as have several Irish names, with the recent increase in the use of Celtic names.

Ava

To many older people the name Ava, pronounced so that the first syllable rhymes with *hay*, is associated with the film actress Ava Gardner. However, the name has become popular with Scottish parents recently and was ranked in the top ten most popular girls' names in Scotland for 2009. The name is of uncertain origin. It may well be Germanic in origin, although a connection with the Latin word for a bird, *avis*, has been suggested. It may be a variant of the name **Eva**.

Barbara

Barbara has its origin in a Greek word meaning 'strange' or 'foreign'. The name became popular in Christian countries from stories of the third-century saint St Barbara, although doubt has been cast on her existence.

Beth

Beth is a short form of the name **Elizabeth**.

Betsy

Betsy is a short form of the name **Elizabeth**, a name which, together with its several short forms, has had a long-lasting popularity in the English-speaking countries of the world, including Scotland. Betsy was once particularly popular in Scotland and was often used as a first name in its own right. The Gaelic form is Beitidh.

See **Elizabeth**.

Betty

see **Elizabeth**

Brenda

Brenda, a name derived from the Old Norse word *brandr*, meaning a 'sword', was once particularly common in Shetland.

Brooke

Brooke, which can be applied either to males or females, has its origin in the word *brook,* meaning a stream, which is Old English in origin. The name is sometimes spelt **Brook**, like the stream.

Brooke as a girl's name has been popularized by the actress Brooke Shields.

Caitlin

This is an Irish name, rather than a native Scottish one, being an Irish form of **Kathleen** or **Catherine**. However, there is a close connection between Ireland and Scotland and Caitlin has become increasingly popular in Scotland, especially recently when Celtic names have become so much in vogue.

See **Catherine**.

Cameron

see **Cameron** *in* **Boys' Names**

Cara

Cara appears in the top fifty in recent lists of most popular girls' names in Scotland. It is derived from the Italian word *cara,* meaning 'beloved' or 'dear one', originally the feminine form of the Latin *carus*.

Caroline, Carol

The name Caroline derives from Carolus, the Latin or Italian form of **Charles**. The name is often shortened to **Carol** which is now a name in its own right. The names **Carrie** and **Carly** are diminutive forms and both of these are sometimes found as names in their own right.

Catherine

Catherine is of uncertain origin, but, at an early stage, it became associated with the Greek word *katharos* meaning 'pure'. This connection led to the spelling Katharine, although Catherine, with the occasional variant Catharine, is more common in Scotland. Catherine was the name of a saint who was tortured on a spiked wheel (the source of the firework Catherine wheel). The name is thought to have been brought to Scotland by people returning from the Crusades. The name has several diminutive forms including **Kate** and **Katie** and these are both now names in their own right.

See **Katie**.

Catriona

Catriona is the Gaelic form of the name **Catherine**. Robert Louis Stevenson did much to popularize the name when he made it the title of one of his novels in 1893 and the name has remained popular in Scotland. Catriona, which appears in other countries in various forms such as Katrina or Katarina, is usually pronounced in Scotland with the stress on the letter *i,* pronounced as *ee*, although it is sometime pronounced to rhyme with Fiona with the stress on the first syllable *Cat*. **Trina** is now a common diminutive form and it is sometimes used as first name in its own right.

Charlotte

Like **Caroline**, Charlotte is a feminine form of **Charles**. The name came to Britain in the early seventeenth century and was popularized by Queen Charlotte, wife of King George III. Its popularity has increased again recently with the general trend towards older names, such as Sophie and Emma. **Charlie** is a diminutive form which is sometimes used as a first name in its own right.

Chloe

Chloe is Greek in origin and means 'green shoot'. According to legend, she was the wife of Daphnis, a Sicilian shepherd who is said to have invented pastoral poetry. The name has recently become popular throughout the UK, including Scotland, appearing in the top ten in recent lists of most popular girls' names in Scotland.

Christian, Christina, Christine

Christian was once a popular female first name in Scotland, it being the name of a sister of Robert the Bruce. The Gaelic form of Christian is Cairistine. As elsewhere, Christian was also used as a male first name. Christian often later became **Christina** and then **Christine**. The Scandinavian form of Christian and Christine is **Kirsten** and this has become popular in Scotland where the shortened form **Kirsty** has become even more popular. The usual short forms of **Christine** – **Chrissie** and **Chris** – are found in Scotland, as elsewhere, but the short form **Teenie** is peculiar to Scotland. **Tina**, another short from of Christine, is sometimes used as a first name in its own right.

Clara, Claire, Clare

Clare is a form of **Clara**, derived from the feminine form of the Latin word *clarus* meaning 'clear' or 'bright'. The name became particularly popular in Scotland in the later part of the twentieth century. **Claire** is an alternative version of the name and this is the French form.

Clementine

Clementine, derived from the Latin word *clemens* meaning 'mild' or 'merciful', was once very popular in Scotland, especially among parents who were staunch Jacobite supporters. This is because the Old Pretender, James Stewart, was married to Clementine Sobieski, granddaughter of the King of Poland, James and Clementine being the parents of Charles Edward Stewart, Bonnie Prince Charles. The popularity of the name did not last very long.

Corin, Corinne

Corin as a female name was originally a diminutive form of **Corinne**, the French form of the Greek word *korinna,* meaning a 'maiden', but it is now a first name in its own right. It is sometimes thought to be Irish in origin and this could be a reason it is being more widely used, given the general increase in popularity of names of Celtic origin.

Deirdre

Deirdre, which is Gaelic in origin, is the name of a character famous in Irish legend. Of great beauty, Deirdre is said to have left her native Ireland to settle in Argyll with her husband and his two brothers. They were lured back to Ireland under false pretences and the three men were killed. Deirdre was devastated and took her own life. The name Deirdre has long been popular in Ireland, but its relative popularity in Scotland is much more recent.

Diana, Diane

Diana was the Roman goddess of the moon and of hunting. The name increased in popularity with the rise in fame of Princess Diana, who married Prince Charles, heir to the British throne. **Diane** is an alternative form and both names are often shortened to **Di**.

Dorothy

Dorothy, together with its earlier form **Dorothea**, is Greek in origin and means 'gift of God'. The name was found in Scotland, as in England, from the fifteenth century and became very popular before gradually falling out of favour. It regained its popularity at the end of the nineteenth century, but went out of fashion around the 1960s. The name has various diminutive forms, including **Dot** and **Dolly**.

Effie

see **Euphemia**

Eileen

see **Aileen**

Eilidh

Eilidh is a Gaelic form of **Helen**. Its appeal in Scotland has increased with the rise in popularity generally of Celtic names.

Eithne, Ethne

Eithne is a Irish female first name, pronounced *eth-nee* and now used in Scotland. Derived from the Gaelic word *aodhnait,* meaning 'little fire', Eithne was the name of the Irish mother of St Columba. It is sometimes now spelt **Ethne**.

Eleanor

Eleanor is Greek in origin and means 'shining light'. It is a form of Helen. The name is thought to have been introduced to England, and then later made its way to Scotland, because of Eleanor of Aquitaine (1122-1204), who married Henry II of England. A rarer spelling of Eleanor is **Elinor**. **Ellie** is a common diminutive form. **Eleanora** and **Leonora** are more formal forms. *See* **Helen** *and* **Ellie**.

Elizabeth

Elizabeth with its many and various short forms such as **Betty**, **Betsy**, **Bess**, **Bessie**, **Liz**, **Lizzie**, **Lisa** and **Libby** has enjoyed long-term popularity in Scotland as well as in many other countries of the world. Hebrew in origin, Elizabeth means 'oath of god'. It was the name of the mother of John the Baptist and this biblical connection established its popularity. The popularity of the name increased in Britain when Queen Elizabeth was born in 1926, being crowned queen in 1953, but then decreased. *See* **Betsy** *and* **Elspeth**.

Ella

Ella is derived from an old Germanic word meaning 'all'. It was probably brought to England, and then Scotland, by the French during the Norman Conquest. It is sometimes used as a diminutive form of **Isabella** or **Isobel**. It is also used as a diminutive form of **Ellen**, **Helen** and **Eleanor**.

Ellen

Ellen is a form of **Helen** and so is derived from a Greek word meaning 'bright'. The name has become a first name in its own right and it has enjoyed particular popularity in Scotland. **Ellie** can be a diminutive form of the name.
See **Helen**.

Ellie

Ellie can be a diminutive form of several names such as **Eleanor**, **Ellen**, **Isobel** or **Isabella**. Nowadays it is frequently found as a name in its own right and, as such, it is gaining popularity.

Elsie

Elsie is a form of **Elizabeth**, and, as such, means 'oath of god'. It can also be a form of **Elspeth**, itself a form of **Elizabeth**. Sometimes Elsie is used as a female first name in its own right, but, whatever its origin, it is not nearly as popular in Scotland as it once was.

Elspeth

Elspeth, which was formerly often shortened to **Elspet** and sometimes to **Eppie**, is a popular form of **Elizabeth** in Scotland.
See **Elizabeth**.

Emily

Emily was originally a diminutive form of the name **Emilia**, a feminine form of Aemilius, a Roman clan name meaning a 'rival' or 'emulator'.

Emilia was recorded in Scotland in the seventeenth century. Emily later became a forename in its own right. Relatively popular in the nineteenth century, it faded from use until the recent resurgence of old Victorian names. Its popularity is now such that it appears in the top ten in recent lists of most popular girls' names in Scotland.

Emma

Emma is German in origin and means 'universal' or 'entire'. It was popularized by the author Jane Austen who made it the title of one of her novels in 1815. It has its origins in Normandy, the name probably having been brought to England by Emma, daughter of a Duke of Normandy who married Ethelred the Unready, King of England, in 1002. The name was recorded in Scotland in the late twelfth century, but it did not achieve the height of its popularity until recently. It is in the top ten in recent lists of the most popular girls' names in Scotland.

Erin

Erin, derived from the Gaelic *Eireann*, meaning 'western isle', is a poetic name given to Ireland.

This has become quite a popular female forename in Scotland with the rise in popularity of Celtic names generally. It appears in the top ten in recent lists of most popular girls' names in Scotland.

Esmé, Esmée

Esmé was originally applied to males and was introduced to Scotland in the sixteenth century by Esme Stewart d'Aubigny, Duke of Lennox and a cousin of James VI. His mother was French and the name Esme is thought to be derived from the Old French verb *esmer*, to esteem. The name began to be used of females and gained much more popularity as a girl's name.

Euphemia

Euphemia was once considerably more common in Scotland than elsewhere. Derived from a Greek word indicating 'highly spoken of', Euphemia was the name of a fourth-century martyr, St Euphemia. A common short form of Euphemia in Scotland was **Effie** and this name appears in Walter Scott's well-known novel *The Heart of Midlothian*.

Eve, Eva

Eve is Hebrew in origin being derived from *havvah* meaning 'life-giving'. According to the Bible, Eve was the name of the first woman. **Eva** is a variant spelling of the name, but it was sometimes used in Scotland for the Gaelic name Eubha, a form of the Irish name **Aoife**. Both Eve and Eva have increased in popularity in Scotland in recent years. The diminutive form **Evie** now exists as a first name in its own right.

Fenella

Fenella is the anglicized form of the Gaelic Fionnghal, formed from *fionn*, 'white' and *guala*, 'shoulder'. The Irish form of the Scots Gaelic name is Fionnuala. The name never became really popular in Scotland, having much greater success in Ireland. Fenella has sometimes been associated with **Flora**, a suggestion being that Flora, rather than **Fenella**, was sometimes used to translate Fionnghal (*see* **Flora**). An Irish form of the Gaelic name Fionnuala is often shortened to **Nuala**.

Fiona

Fiona is connected with the Gaelic word *fionn*, 'fair' or 'white'. The creation of the name has been ascribed to James Macpherson (1736-96) who was responsible for the Ossian poems, although references have been found to more ancient names with a similar form. For example, a woman called **Fione** was the wife of Reginald, Lord of the Isles, in the late twelfth century.

Flora

Flora is the name of the Roman goddess of flowers, being derived from the Latin word *flos*, a 'flower'. The name appeared as a female first name in France during the Renaissance, and was introduced to Scotland from there. The name is in general use and not in any way confined to Scotland. However, the popularity of the name in Scotland was increased, particularly among Jacobite families, by Flora Macdonald (1722-90) who helped Prince Charles Edward Stewart (Bonnie Prince Charlie) escape after the defeat of the Jacobites at the Battle of Culloden (1746). It has been suggested that Flora, rather than **Fenella**, was sometimes used to translate Fionnghal.

Frances

Frances is the feminine form of **Francis** (*see* **Boys' Names**). Diminutive forms of this include **Fran** and **Franny**.

Freya

Freya is derived from the Norse goddess of love whose name meant 'female ruler'. The name was once particularly popular in Shetland, but in recent times its popularity has increased in the rest of Scotland and it appears in the top forty in recent lists of most popular girls' names in Scotland.

Georgia

The name **Georgia** first became popular as a girl's name in America, after the state of the name, and this popularity has spread, to some extent, to the UK, including Scotland.

Georgina

Georgina is a feminine form of **George**. The name has been found in Scotland since the early eighteenth century, but the fashion for

using feminine forms of male names has faded
and names such as Georgina are no longer very
common.

See **Ina**.

Gillies

see **Gillies** *in* **Boys' Names**

Grace

Grace is derived from the Latin word *gratia*
meaning 'grace' or 'favour'. The name became
popular in Britain at the time of the Puritans
who named their daughters after several virtuous
qualities such as Faith, Hope, Charity and
Patience. Grace became particularly popular in
Scotland, but faded from common use in the
middle of the twentieth century. In common
with several other older names, it has recently
enjoyed a resurgence in popularity and it appears
in the top twenty in recent lists of most popular
girls' names in Scotland. The Gaelic for Grace is
Giorsail and, because of this, Grace sometimes
became confused with **Grizel**.

Grizel

Grizel was once a popular name in Scotland, being a particularly Scottish form of the name **Griselda**. Griselda became associated with the virtue patience after Boccaccio, the fourteenth-century Italian writer, wrote a story about a wife who showed remarkable patience, despite her husband's extreme attempts to test this. The story was brought to a wider audience in the English-speaking world by Chaucer's retelling of it. Grizel was sometimes shortened to **Gris** and became confused with **Grace**.

Hannah

Hannah is derived from Hebrew and means 'favoured one'. In the Bible Hannah was unable to have a child until God intervened and she had a son, Samuel. The name Hannah was originally not nearly as generally popular in Britain as **Ann**, **Anne** and **Anna**, which are derived from it, although Hannah was particularly popular among Jewish families. However, with the recent resurgence in popularity of old names, including biblical names, Hannah has become much more common and appears in the top twenty in recent lists of most popular girls' names in Scotland.

Harriet

Harriet is an English form of the French name Henriette. It is the feminine form of **Henry** or **Harry** and was quite popular in Scotland before fading from fashion. **Hattie** and **Hettie** are short forms of **Harriet**.

Hazel

The name Hazel has its origin in the tree of the name. It has been used in Scotland since the late nineteenth century.

Heather

Heather, the plant, is traditionally associated with Scotland. The female first name was named after it and became popular in Scotland and elsewhere from the late nineteenth century.

Helen

Helen is derived from a Greek word meaning 'bright' and may be related to *helios*, the Greek word for 'sun'. It was the name given to the beautiful woman, Helen of Troy, who, according to legend, was associated with the start of the Trojan War. The name has long been popular in Scotland, as has the form **Ellen**, being particularly popular in the second half of the nineteenth century and the first part of the twentieth century. **Nellie** is a diminutive from of the name.

See **Eilidh** *and* **Ellen**.

Holly

The name Holly has its origin in the tree of the name. It has been used in Scotland since the beginning of the twentieth century and has become particularly popular in recent years. **Hollie** is a recent alternative spelling.

Ina

Ina is used as a suffix to make the female forms of some male first names, as in Georgina from George. In Scotland Ina came to be used sometimes as a female first name in its own right, the initial letter sometimes being pronounced to rhyme with *me* and sometimes being pronounced to rhyme with *eye*. The name has declined in popularity.

Innes

Innes, more commonly a Scottish surname, is sometimes used as a male first name and sometimes as a female first name in Scotland. It is derived from a place name, Innes being an island.

Iona

Iona is named after the island of Iona where St Columba founded a monastery in 563.

Irene

Irene is derived from the Greek word *eirene* meaning 'peace'. The name was particularly popular in Scotland in the first part of the twentieth century, but has faded considerably since then.

Ishbel

Ishbel is a form of **Iseabail**, the Gaelic form of **Isobel**, and the alternative spelling **Isabel**.
See **Isobel**, **Isabel**.

Isla

Isla is a Scottish place name, being the name of a river and glen in Perthshire, and it is possible that the first name Isla is derived from that. However, it may be derived from the Hebridean island of **Islay**. The island has given its name to the Scottish first name **Islay**, which has been used for both males and females. Isla appears in the top twenty in recent lists of most popular girls' names in Scotland.

Islay

see **Isla**

Isobel, Isabel

Isobel and Isabel are derived from **Isabella**, the Italian and Spanish forms of **Elizabeth**. The name Isabella, as well as its derivative forms, has been much used in Scotland. Diminutive forms of the names include **Bella**, **Ella** and **Ellie**, which often now appear in their own right as first names, and **Isa** and **Izzy**.
See **Ella** and **Ellie**.

Jacqueline

Jacqueline is derived from the feminine form of the French name Jacques which is the equivalent of the English **James**. The name was particularly popular in Scotland in the mid-twentieth century, but faded from popularity after that. The diminutive form **Jackie** is now used as a name in its own right.

Jane

Jane, like **Jean**, is a common feminine form of **John**. The Latin form of the name is Johanna and the Gaelic form of Jane is Sine, anglicized as **Sheena**.

Janet

Janet was originally a pet form of **Jane**. Janet then became an extremely popular name in Scotland in its own right, although its popularity has waned considerably. Janet gave rise to the pet forms **Jenny**, **Jessie**, **Jinty** and **Netta**, although some of these became first names in their own right. **Jonet** was an early form of the name. *See* **Sinead**, **Seonaid**.

Jean

Jean is a feminine form of **John** and it enjoyed great popularity in Scotland for a long time, although its popularity has gradually waned. Jean has the diminutive form **Jeanie**. The Gaelic form of Jean is Sine.
See **Sheena**.

Jennifer

Jennifer probably has connections with the Welsh name Gwenhwyfar meaning 'fair, smooth and yielding'. Originally a Cornish name, Jennifer was particularly popular in Scotland from the 1950s until the late 1970s, but its popularity faded. The diminutive form **Jenny** is also used as a first name in its own right.

Jenny

Jenny is usually considered to be a short form of **Jennifer**. In Scotland, however, it was once a form of **Janet**.

Jessica, Jesse

The name was popularized by Shakespeare when he named Shylock's daughter **Jessica** in his play *The Merchant of Venice* (1596). Shakespeare is thought to have based the name on the biblical character Iscah, daughter of Haran in the Old Testament book in the Bible. Because Shylock was Jewish, the name Jessica was once considered to be Jewish. The name was not particularly popular in Scotland, the popular name **Jessie**, being, in Scotland, a short form of the name **Janet**. However, Jessica appears in the top twenty in recent lists of most popular girls' names in Scotland.

Joan

Like Jean, Joan is a feminine form of **John** although the name was originally applied also to men. The name was often spelt **Johan**, more recently becoming **Johann**, and pronounced as two syllables. The forms **Joanne** and **Joanna** are now more popular. The Gaelic form of Joan is Seonag.

Jodie

see **Judith**

Josephine

Josephine is the feminine form of **Joseph**. The name was quite popular in Scotland in the early part of the twentieth century, but its popularity waned. The diminutive forms **Jo** and **Josie** are also found as first names in their own right.

Joyce

The derivation of Joyce is uncertain, although it may be Celtic in origin. The name, which originally often took the form of **Josse** and was applied to males, was the name of a Breton saint, Latinized as **Jodocus**. It was quite popular in Scotland in the middle of the twentieth century, but its use has faded since then.

Judith

Judith is Jewish in origin, being derived from *Yehudith*, a Jewish woman, and Latinized as Juditha. The Gaelic form of the name is Siobhan. Originally a name particularly favoured by

Jewish people, Judith was fairly rare in Scotland until the seventeenth century and it has never enjoyed widespread popularity. The diminutive forms **Judy** and **Jodie** are often used as names in their own right, **Jodie** becoming particularly popular recently.

Julia, Julie

Julia is the feminine form of the Latin name Julius which means 'bearded' or 'downy'. The French form of the name, **Julie**, is more popular in Scotland. In Scotland Julia sometimes had an alternative derivation; **Giles** as a female name probably eventually developing into Julia.
See **Giles** *in* **Boys' Names**.

Karen

Karen is a diminutive form of the Scandinavian name Katerina, a form of **Catherine**. It came into use in the 1930s and has been popular in Scotland since the middle of the twentieth century.
See **Catriona**.

Kate

Kate was originally a form of **Catherine**, a name of uncertain origin, but thought to be connected with the Greek word *katharos*, meaning 'pure'. Kate has been popular from medieval times, but in recent times the form **Katie** has become more popular.

See **Catherine**.

Kathleen

Kathleen, like **Caitlin**, is an Irish form of **Catherine**. Because of the long connection between Ireland and Scotland, with many Irish families coming to live in Scotland, **Kathleen** also became commonly used in Scotland.

See **Catherine**.

Katie

Katie, like **Kate**, was originally a form of **Catherine**, of uncertain origin, but thought to be connected with the Greek word *katharos*, meaning 'pure'. Both Kate and Katie are now used as popular first names in their own right. Katie appears in the top ten in recent lists of most popular girls' names in Scotland.

Kay

As a female first name Kay, with the alternative spelling **Kaye**, is often a diminutive form of **Katharine**, **Kathleen** or other names beginning with the letter 'K', although it can be a first name in its own right. It may well have been popularized for a time by the actress Kay Kendall (1926-59).

Kayla

Kayla appears in the top fifty in recent lists of most popular girls' names in Scotland. Its origin is uncertain. It may be derived from **Michaela**, a feminine form of **Michael**. Alternatively, it may sometimes be a form of **Kayleigh**.

Kayleigh

The name Kayleigh may have been popularized in Scotland by the British rock group Marillion who, with lead singer Fish, recorded a successful song of the name in 1985. The name may be based on the name **Kay** or it may sometimes be a form of **Kylie**.

Kelly

Although Kelly is a common Irish surname, there are also people of the name originating in Scotland, particularly from Fife and Angus. Recently it has begun to be used both as a female and male first name. The spelling **Kellie** is also used.

Kerry

The name Kerry has obvious connections with Ireland since it is the name of an Irish county. Since the second part of the twentieth century it has been used as a girl's name. It is possible that it came to Scotland from Australia where it was also used as a male first name. The name may have connections with **Carrie**, a diminutive form of **Caroline**.

Kiera, Keira

Kiera and Keira are feminine forms of **Kieran**. Keira appears in the top thirty in recent list of most popular girls' names in Scotland.

Kirsten, Kirsty

see **Christian**

Kylie

The girl's name **Kylie** was popularized by the Australian singer Kylie Minogue. The origin of the name is uncertain. It may have connections with the surname and male first name **Kyle**. It may also have connections with the Australian Aboriginal word for 'boomerang'.

Laura

Laura is Latin in origin and may be a shortened from of **Laurencia**, a feminine form of **Lawrence**. The name was popularized by the Italian poet Petrarch who wrote love sonnets to a woman of the name. Laura was brought to England in the fifteenth century and the name spread to Scotland.

Lauren

Lauren may be a feminine form of the masculine name **Lawrence**. Alternatively, it may be a form of the name **Laurel**. It was popular in America before becoming so in England and Scotland, its American popularity probably having something to do with the actress Lauren Bacall. It is now especially popular in Scotland.

Leah

Leah is Hebrew in origin and means 'tender-eyed'. In the Bible, Leah is the sister of Rachel and one of the wives of Jacob. The name was introduced to England by the Puritans in the late sixteenth century and it spread to Scotland. It was never particularly popular until recently when there was a surge of interest in Old Testament names. Leah appears in the top twenty in recent lists of most popular girls' names in Scotland.

Lesley

Lesley is the feminine form of **Leslie**, although the distinction between the use of Leslie for men and Lesley for women has become blurred over the years.

Lily

This name's popularity in Scotland may well be due to the fact that it is a flower name, derived from the Latin *lilium*, the lily being a symbol of purity. Originally, it may have been a diminutive form of **Lilias**, a popular Scottish variation of **Lilian**, derived from Liliana, the Italian form of Lily.

Linda

Linda was originally used as a diminutive form of several names such as Belinda or Rosalind, the *-linda* element perhaps being derived from a Germanic word *linde*, meaning 'serpent'. Linda came to be a popular name in its own right, becoming particularly common in Scotland in the late 1950s, but its popularity has since faded somewhat.

Lindsay

Lindsay originally appeared as a Scottish surname. It came into being in the twelfth century when a Norman baron of the name de Lindsay accompanied David I back to Scotland from England. The name later became both a male and female first name, although nowadays the name is mostly given to girls. The name has acquired various alternative spellings such as **Lindsey**, **Linsey** and **Lyndsey**.

Lorna

The female first name Lorna sounds as though it would be a female form of **Lorne** or at least connected with it, but this seems not to be the case. Lorna is a relatively modern name, having been invented by author R. D. Blackmore (1825-1900) when he gave it to the heroine of his novel *Lorna Doone*.

Louise

Louise is the French feminine form of **Louis**. **Louisa** is the Latin feminine form of Louis and was popular in Scotland in the eighteenth and the nineteenth century. However, the spelling Louise overtook Louisa and was very popular in the late 1970s.

Lucy

Lucy is the English form of **Lucia**, the feminine form of **Lucius** meaning 'light'. Traditionally, Lucius and Lucia were used to name children born at dawn. The name Lucy was once popular throughout England and Scotland, but its popularity faded in the nineteenth century. Recently it has enjoyed a resurgence of its popularity and it appears in the top ten in recent lists of most popular girls' names in Scotland.

Maggie

see **Margaret**

Mairi

Mairi is a form of **Mhairi**, the Gaelic for **Mary**. *See* **Mhairi**.

Maisie

Maisie is a Scottish form of **Margaret** or **Marjorie**. It is probably formed from the Gaelic for Marjorie, Marsaili. It is sometimes found in the form of **Mysie**, especially in speech, although this is now considered to be old-fashioned.

Margaret

Margaret, although not of Scottish origin, has enjoyed great popularity in Scotland over the centuries. It is thought to be Persian in origin, meaning 'pearl'. Originally Margaret owed its great popularity in Scotland to the fact that it was the name of a much admired and loved queen, Queen Margaret. She was a Saxon princess who came to Scotland from England and married King Malcolm III. In Scotland, as elsewhere, there are several different forms of Margaret, such as **Margo**, **Margery**, **Madge** and **Peggy**. **Maisie** is a particularly Scottish form. **Maggie** and **Meg** are common diminutive forms.

Margery

Margery is a form of **Margaret**. An alternative from is **Marjorie**. **Marge** is a diminutive form. *See* **Maisie**.

Maria, Marie

Maria is the Latin form of **Mary** and is associated with the Virgin Mary, mother of Jesus. The name has long been popular in several countries in Europe, such as Italy and Spain, and it has been used in Scotland as an alternative to Mary, although **Marie**, the French form of **Mary**, has enjoyed greater popularity in Scotland.

Marion

A diminutive form of **Mary** or **Marie**, the French form of Mary, **Marian**, a form of Marion, being an adjective used to refer to the name Mary, particularly the Virgin Mary or a monarch called Mary. The name was popular in the Middle Ages and was quite popular in the latter part of the nineteenth century and in the first part of the twentieth century, but it has faded from fashion since.

Mary

Mary, although it has no special Scottish connections, has been an extremely popular name in Scotland. Its popularity was no doubt originally a result of the name's biblical connections, Mary being the mother of Jesus. The Gaelic form of Mary is **Mhairi** and this, together with the alternative form **Mairi**, has become very popular in Scotland. **Molly** was originally a form of Mary, although it has now become a name in its own right.

Maureen

Maureen is a form of the Irish name Mairin, diminutive form of Maire, the Irish Gaelic form of **Mary**. It was particularly popular in Scotland in the middle part of the twentieth century, but it faded from fashion in the later part of the twentieth century.

Megan

A Welsh name which arose as a pet form of **Meg**, a diminutive form of **Margaret** which means 'pearl'. The use of Megan was originally restricted to Wales, but its popularity has recently spread to other countries. It appears in the top twenty in recent lists of most popular girls' names in Scotland.
See **Margaret**.

Mhairi

Mhairi is the Gaelic form of **Mary**. It has become very popular throughout Scotland and elsewhere with the recent increase in interest in Celtic names. The alternative form **Mairi** is also popular and, to some extent, avoids the spelling problem.

Mia

Mia appears in the top thirty in recent lists of most popular girls' names in Scotland. Various derivations for the name have been suggested, including a shortened version of **Maria** or the Italian word for the personal pronoun 'mine'. The name was popularized by the actress Mia Farrow.

Millie

Millie appears in the top forty in recent lists of most popular girls' names in Scotland. It is now a first name in its own right, but it was originally a diminutive form of **Mildred**. Mildred is Old English in origin, being derived from *milde* meaning 'mild' or 'gentle' and *thyrthe* meaning 'power'. The name was popular in the Middle Ages and enjoyed a period of relative popularity in Britain in the early nineteenth century, although it was less popular in Scotland.

Moira

Moira is a form of the Irish Gaelic name Maire, the equivalent of **Mary**. It was especially popular in Scotland in the middle of the twentieth century.

Molly

Molly was originally found as a pet form of **Mary**. Although not Irish in origin, the name became particularly associated with Ireland. Molly is now a first name in its own right and popular in Scotland.

Morag

Morag was originally a diminutive of the Gaelic word *mor*, meaning 'great'. It became a popular female first name, originally in the Highlands. The anglicized form is **Sarah**, although it is not clear why.
See **Sarah**.

Morgan

Morgan was originally an ancient Celtic male first name. The derivation is uncertain, but a possible meaning is 'sea-bright'. Morgan became a surname, most popular in Wales, but it was recorded as a male first name in Scotland and as a surname in the early fifteenth century. Later it became a female first name.

Nancy

Nancy is often used as a pet form of **Ann**, although in Scotland it has frequently been used as a form of **Agnes**. It has become a name in its own right.

Nicola, Nicole

Nicole is the French feminine form of **Nicholas**. The Italian form **Nicola** came to England in the thirteenth century and spread to Scotland. Later, it was overtaken in popularity by the form Nicole. **Nicky**, **Nikky**, **Nikki** and **Niki** are diminutive forms which have become names in their own right.

Niamh

Niamh is Celtic in origin and is pronounced *neev*. Meaning 'radiance' or 'brightness', the name has long been popular in Ireland, but has recently also become popular in Scotland. There is a well-known Irish legend about a very beautiful woman known as Niamh of the Golden Hair who was a daughter of Manannan, the god of the sea.

Nora

Nora is a diminutive form of **Eleanor**, **Eleanora** or **Leonara** (*see* **Eleanor**) which was relatively popular in Scotland in the first part of the twentieth century. It is sometimes spelt **Norah**.

Nuala

Nuala is Celtic in origin and is pronounced *noo-la*. A shortened form of the Irish Gaelic name Fionnuala, Nuala has been in common use in Ireland for a long time. It has only recently come to be used much in Scotland with the increase in interest in names of Celtic origin.
See **Fenella**.

Olivia, Olive

Olivia is linguistically connected with the olive tree, traditionally associated with peace. The name has recently become popular in Scotland and appears in the top ten in recent lists of most popular girls' names. The name **Olive**, which is related to Olivia, appeared in England in the twelfth century, often taking the form Oliff. It became popular in Britain towards the end of the nineteenth century when names derived from botanical terms became common.

Paige

Paige was originally a surname. It is a variant spelling of *page*, which is French in origin and means 'young helper'. Around the middle of the twentieth century it began to be used as a female first name, especially in America, and occasionally as a male first name. Its popularity has now spread to Scotland.

Pamela

The name Pamela was invented by the Elizabethan poet Sir Philip Sidney (1554-86) for a character in his romance *Arcadia*. The name was made more famous and popular by another writer, Samuel Richardson (1689-1761), who used it both as the name of a novel

(1740) and the name of the virtuous servant girl who features in the novel. Pamela was quite popular in Scotland until relatively recently but it has been overtaken by other names. **Pam** is a common diminutive form.

Patricia

Patricia is a feminine form of **Patrick**. The name was popular in the first part of the twentieth century but its popularity has been overtaken by various other names. Pat is a common diminutive form. **Trish** and **Trisha** are more modern diminutive forms and they are now used as first names in their own right.

Pauline

Pauline is a feminine form of **Paul**. Pauline was quite popular in Scotland around the middle of the twentieth century, but it has faded from popularity. **Paula** is another feminine form of Paul which was popular in Scotland for a time.

Rachel

Rachel is Hebrew in origin and means 'ewe', a symbol of gentleness. It has biblical connections, being the name of the second wife of Jacob and the mother of Joseph and Benjamin. The name became popular in Scotland after the Reformation, but its popularity faded in the nineteenth century. With the recent resurgence in old names, including Old Testament names, Rachel has become so popular in Scotland that it appears in the top twenty in recent lists of most popular girls' names.

Rebecca

Rebecca is a biblical name, Rebecca being the name of the wife of Isaac and the mother of Esau and Jacob. The name is assumed to be Hebrew in origin, but it is of uncertain derivation. Various linguistic connections have been suggested including the verb to tie or bind and the verb to fatten or feed up. The name was particularly popular with the Puritans, but gradually waned in popularity towards the end of the nineteenth century. With the recent resurgence in old names, including Old Testament names, Rebecca has become so popular in Scotland that it appears in top twenty in recent lists of most popular names. **Becky** is a common diminutive form of **Rebecca** and this is now frequently found as a first name in its own right.

Robin, Robyn

Robin was originally used as a male name in Scotland as a form of **Robert**. In recent years it has become a female first name, its popularity first arising in America. It is now commonly spelt **Robyn**.

Rona, Rhona

Rona came into use in Scotland in the later part of the nineteenth century, but its origin is unclear. It may be named after a Scottish island of the name, the possible derivation of which is Norse *hraun-ey* meaning 'rough island'. Certainly, the names of other Scottish islands have become first names, including **Islay**. Alternatively, it may be a feminine form of the male first name **Ronan**. The name **Rhona** is likely to be a form of Rona.

Rose

The name Rose is usually associated with the name of the flower. Flower names, including Rose, became popular in Scotland, as elsewhere, in the later part of the nineteenth century. However, the name Rose was common long before then and it may have its origins in the Germanic word *hros*, a 'horse'. The Normans may have brought the name to England in the form of Roese or Rhoese.

Rosemary

The name Rosemary is derived from the aromatic shrub of the name. The name became popular in the later part of the nineteenth century when flower and plant names became fashionable, although the name dates from the middle of the eighteenth century. The name of the shrub is derived from the Latin word *ros*, meaning 'dew', and the Latin word *marinus*, meaning 'of the sea'.

Rowan

Rowan was originally used both as a male first name and a female one in Scotland. More recently, the female name has become more common. The origin of the name Rowan is uncertain. It may be derived from the tree of the name which has red berries. Alternatively, it may be derived from the Gaelic word *ruadhan* meaning 'little red one'.

Ruby

Ruby became rather old-fashioned, but there has been a resurgence in its popularity in Scotland. It is derived from the red-coloured jewel of the name.

Ruth

Ruth is a famous biblical character and one of the books of the Old Testament is named after her. The origin of the name is uncertain, although it is thought to be of Hebrew derivation. The name became quite popular after the Reformation and was frequently used by the Puritans in the seventeenth century. They liked abstract names relating to virtues, such as faith, charity and hope, and probably connected Ruth with the word *ruth* meaning 'pity'.

Samantha, Sam

There is some uncertainty about the origin of the name Samantha, although it is generally accepted to be a feminine form of **Samuel**. The name was used in the southern states of America, in both the black and white population, long before it became known in Britain in the middle of the twentieth century. It became very popular in Scotland in the later part of the twentieth century. Samantha, like **Samuel,** is sometimes shortened to **Sam** and this has now become a first name in its own right.

Sandra

Sandra is a short form of **Alexandra**, the feminine form of **Alexander**. It was fairly popular in Scotland in the mid-twentieth century, but it faded from fashion after that.

Sarah

Sarah is Hebrew in origin and means 'princess'. It has biblical connections, being the name of the wife of Abraham and the mother of Isaac. Her name was originally **Sarai**, but it is said to have been changed on the advice of God. The name

Sarah enjoyed a good deal of popularity once but this began to fade in the middle of the twentieth century. However, Sarah's popularity has increased with the resurgence of the old names, including Old Testament names. It appears in the top twenty in recent lists of most popular girls' names in Scotland. **Sara** is an alternative form of Sarah, although this is often pronounced to rhyme with *star*, rather than rhyming with *stare*, as Sarah usually does. **Sally** was originally a diminutive form of **Sarah**, although this has also been a common name in its own right since the eighteenth century. The Gaelic name **Morag** was sometimes anglicized as Sarah.

Senga
see **Agnes**

Sharon

Sharon has its origin in a Hebrew word meaning 'plain', a reference to a fertile plain located between Jaffa and Mount Carmel. The place is referred to in the Bible in the expression 'rose of Sharon' in the *Song of Songs* and in the phrase 'Sharon's dewy rose' in a well-known hymn.

The name, which originally could be applied to either females or males, began to be used in the seventeenth century, especially by the Puritans. It became popular in Scotland in the later part of the twentieth century, but is no longer as fashionable.

Sheena

Sheena is the anglicized spelling of Sine which is Gaelic for **Jean**.

Sheila

Sheila has enjoyed a steady popularity in Scotland over the years. It is an anglicization of Sile, the Gaelic form of Celia.

Sinead, Seonaid, Shona

Sinead, pronounced *shinade*, is a form of Janet and has long been popular in Ireland. It has become popular in Scotland, especially following the increased interest in Celtic names. The Scots Gaelic form of the name is **Seonaid** and both spellings now exist in Scotland. The anglicized form of the Gaelic name is **Shona**.

Siobhan

Siobhan, pronounced *shiv-awn*, is an Irish form of Joan or Jane, female forms of the popular male first name **John**. It is a very popular name in Ireland and has recently become well liked in Scotland, following the increased interest in Celtic names.

Skye

Skye, which is derived from the famous Hebridean island of the name, has only relatively recently been used as a female first name.

Sophie, Sophia

Sophie is a form of **Sophia** which is Greek in origin and means 'wisdom'. The name came to England from central Europe and then spread to Scotland. Sophia was quite common in Scotland from the early seventeenth century, but, in modern times, the variant **Sophie** has become much more common and has recently become extremely popular. It appears in the top ten in recent lists of most popular girls' names in Scotland, frequently at the top of the list.

Susan, Susanna

Susan was originally a short form of **Susanna** although it became a first name in its own right. Susanna is derived from a Hebrew word meaning 'lily', and later meaning 'rose'. Susanna is a biblical character whose story is told in the *Apocrypha* in the Bible. She was wrongly convicted of adultery by the Elders and condemned to death, but she was saved by Daniel who exposed the lies of the Elders. The name Susan was particularly popular in Scotland in the mid-twentieth century, but has faded from fashion since then. Short forms include **Sue** and **Susie**, which are now sometimes used as first names in their own right.

Teresa, Theresa

The origin of the name is uncertain. There are two popular theories. One is that the name is derived from the Greek island of Thera. The other is that it is derived from the Greek word *therizein*, meaning to 'reap'. In Scotland the name became popular, particular in Roman Catholic families, because of a French saint, St Therese of Lisieux. Diminutive forms include **Tess**, **Tessa** and **Terry** which are sometimes now first names in their own right.

See **Tracy**.

Tracy, Tracey

Tracy, with the alternative form of **Tracey**, is probably of Norman origin, being called after a place name in northern France. It was originally a surname and a male first name, later becoming mainly a female first name. The name became popular in Scotland in the later part of the twentieth century, but it is no longer as fashionable. The name is sometimes regarded as a diminutive form of **Teresa**.

Valerie

Valerie is derived from the Roman name Valeria which is the feminine form of the Roman clan name Valerius, derived from the Latin word *valere* meaning to be 'well' or 'strong'. The name Valeria came to England from France and became Valerie. It was at its most popular in Scotland in the late 1950s. **Val** is a diminutive form of the name.

Victoria, Vicky, Vikki

Victoria is derived from the Latin word for 'victory'. The name was known in Scotland around 1600. Surprisingly, it was not particularly popular during the reign of Queen Victoria, which ended in 1901 and it was not until the middle of the twentieth century that the name became popular. Nowadays the diminutive forms **Vicky** and **Vikki** have become first names in their own right.

Vivien

Vivien is derived from the French name **Vivienne**. It is the name of a character in Arthurian legend, described as a 'wily harlot', who tried to seduce King Arthur and became Merlin's mistress. Vivien enjoyed a relatively brief spell of popularity in Scotland around the 1940s because of the popularity of actress Vivien Leigh in her role as Scarlett O'Hara in the ever-popular film *Gone with the Wind* (1939). Her name was originally Vivian, which is also a male first name, but she changed it to Vivien.

Wendy

The name Wendy was invented by Scottish playwright J. M. Barrie for one of the Darling family in his popular play *Peter Pan* (1904).

Winifred

There is some uncertainty about the origin of the name Winifred, although it is generally thought to be Welsh in origin, derived from Gwenfrewi, meaning 'blessed reconciliation'. However, it may also have connections with the Old English words *wynn*, 'joy', and *frith* 'peace'. The name has been in use since the sixteenth century and enjoyed a brief period of popularity in Scotland in the late nineteenth century and the first part of the twentieth century. **Winnie** is a common diminutive form of the name.

Zoe

Zoe is derived from a Greek word meaning 'life'. Although the name was popular with the early Christians, it did not become used in Britain until around the middle of the twentieth century.

Boys' Names

Aaron

Until very recently, Aaron was rarely found in Scotland, although it was recorded as early as the fourth century in Britain. However, the name has greatly increased in popularity and it appears in recent top ten lists of most popular boys' names in Scotland. Aaron is Hebrew in origin and means 'great height'. Aaron was the brother of Moses, according to the Old Testament of the Bible.

Adam, Adamnan

Adam, better known as the name of the first man on Earth, according to biblical sources, has been used in Scotland since early times. The name was once particularly popular among Gaelic speakers, the Gaelic form of the name being Adhamb. However, it appears in the top twenty in recent lists of most popular boys' names in Scotland. Adam, derived from the Hebrew word for 'red', and perhaps once used to refer to someone of a ruddy or florid complexion, has given rise to several surnames such as MacAdam. Whether or not **Adamnan**, the name given to a seventh-century saint and biographer of St Columba, is connected with **Adam** is open to dispute.

Aeneas

Aeneas is a Greek name meaning 'praiseworthy'. Since it is the name of a Trojan hero whose legendary exploits were written about by Virgil, its presence in a list of Scottish first names may seem very strange. For an explanation *see* **Angus**.

Aeth

see **Aidan**

Aidan, Aiden

Aidan is a male first name derived from **Aed** or **Aeth**, a Gaelic name meaning 'fire', and later spelt **Aoth** or **Aodh**. There are two famous Aidans in history. One was king of the Dalriada Scots who died around 606 and who was inaugurated as king by St Columba on Iona. The other was a monk from Iona who founded a monastery at Lindisfarne, becoming Bishop of Lindisfarne and dying in 651. Aidan, and its alternative form **Aiden**, has enjoyed an increase in popularity recently. **Aodh** was sometimes anglicized in Scotland as **Hugh**.

Alan, Allan, Allen

Alan, which also has the forms **Allan** and **Allen**, has long been a favourite Scottish male first name, although it is by no means restricted to Scotland. It is Celtic in origin, the Gaelic form being Ailean, although the actual history and meaning of the name is uncertain. The name is thought to have originated in Brittany and to have come to Britain at the time of the Norman Conquest. The name is sometimes shortened to **Al**. **Alana** and **Alanna** are modern feminine forms of Alan.

Alasdair, Alastair, Alistair, Alister

Alasdair, together with the forms **Alastair**, **Alistair**, and **Alister**, is the Gaelic form of **Alexander**. The popularity of the name has spread, but the form Alasdair is not common outside Scotland. The name is sometimes shortened to **Al** or **Ally**.

Albert

Albert is Germanic in origin, being derived from a word meaning 'noble, bright'. It is related to the Old English Aethelbeorht, **Ethelbert**. The name

Albert was not common in Britain until after 1840
when Queen Victoria married Prince Albert,
Prince of Saxe-Coburg and Gotha and originally
called Albrecht. The name was relatively popular
in the late nineteenth century and early twentieth
century, but it faded from fashion.

Alexander

Alexander is Greek in origin, meaning 'defender
of men'. The best-known Alexander is, of course,
Alexander the Great (356-323 BC), the famous
conqueror. The name became exceptionally
popular in Scotland because of its connections
with Scottish royalty. Alexander I, a son of
Malcolm Canmore and Queen Margaret, came
to the Scottish throne in 1107 and reigned until
1124. It is thought that he owed his name to the
fact that his mother had been brought up in the
Hungarian court where the name Alexander
would have been familiar. Alexander I's grandson
Alexander II ruled Scotland from 1214 until
1249 and he was succeeded by his son, Alexander
III, who was accidentally killed near Kinghorn
in 1286. By the time of his tragic death the name
Alexander was firmly established in Scotland

and it has gone on being popular, appearing in the top twenty in recent lists of most popular boys' names in Scotland. Alexander has long been frequently shortened to **Sandy** or to **Alex**, **Alec** or **Alick**. These names are sometimes used as first names in their own right. **Alexandra** is the feminine form although, despite its royal connections with Princess Alexandra, this has never been very popular in Scotland.

Andrew

Andrew, derived from the Greek *andros* meaning 'manly', has long been a popular name in Scotland. This is perfectly understandable as Andrew is the name of Scotland's patron saint, St Andrew's Day being celebrated on 30 November. The name has continued to be popular, despite competition from more modern names, and appears in the top twenty in recent lists of most popular boys' names in Scotland. Andrew is often shortened to **Andy** and sometimes to **Drew**, although this later became quite common as a first name in its own right.

Angus

Angus is an ancient name and is derived from an ancient Celtic word meaning 'unique choice', the Gaelic form of the name being Aonghus or Aonghas. The name is recorded at an early date in Ireland, but it then became almost exclusively associated with Scotland, being especially common in the Highlands and the Western Isles. According to tradition, Angus was one of three brothers, the others being **Fergus** and **Lorne**, who, around 503, came from Ireland to Scotland to settle in what became Dalriada. Because of the similarity between the pronunciation of the Gaelic **Aonghus** and the name **Aeneas** the two names became confused and **Aeneas**, surprisingly, became a Scottish name.

Antony, Anthony

Anthony is derived from the Roman clan name Antonius which is of uncertain origin. The spelling **Anthony**, which is now very common, came into being after the Renaissance, perhaps because it was thought that the name was associated with the Greek word *anthos*, meaning 'flower'. The name was particularly popular in

Scotland in the mid-twentieth century. **Tony** is a popular diminutive form of the name and this is now a name in its own right. The feminine form of Antony is **Antonia**, which was popular in Scotland in the later part of the twentieth century.

Archibald, Archie

Archibald is Germanic in origin, conveying qualities such as genuineness, nobility and boldness. It has been suggested that some Gaelic speakers thought that the last syllable of Archibald indicated a lack of hair and, by extension, a monk (because of the tonsure adopted by monks). They, thus, mistakenly used Archibald as a translation of the Gaelic name Gilleasbuig (**Gillespie**). This name, which was popular in Scotland from the twelfth century, means literally 'shaven servant of the bishop', the Gaelic word *gillie* meaning a 'youth' or 'servant'. Archibald became a very popular name in Scotland, apparently having been adopted originally by the Campbell chiefs, but it faded from popularity in the second part of the twentieth century. The name is often shortened to **Archie** and this has become more popular than the parent name.

Arthur

Arthur is of uncertain origin, although it has been suggested that the name is Celtic in origin and that it is related to the Greek word *arktos*, meaning 'bear'. This is not a name that we immediately associate with Scotland, although the surname Macarthur is quite common. However, there is a reference as early as the late sixth century to the existence of the name in Scotland in that Aedan, King of Scots, who died in 606, had a son named Arthur. That the name Arthur is so well-known in Britain generally is due to the legendary King Arthur who founded the Knights of the Round Table and had his court at Camelot.

Benjamin, Ben

Ben is a short form of **Benjamin**, but it is now used as a male first name in its own right. Indeed, Ben is an extremely popular name in Scotland, appearing in the top twenty in recent lists of most popular boys' names in Scotland. **Benjamin** is Hebrew in origin and means 'son of the right hand'. In the Bible, Benjamin was the youngest son of Jacob. It was originally most popular among Jewish families.

Bernard

The name Bernard is Germanic in origin, being derived from words meaning 'hard bear' or 'stern bear'. It came to England after the Norman Conquest. The name was quite popular in Scotland in the 1930s, especially among Roman Catholic families. **Bernie** and **Barney** are short forms of the name.

Brian

The name Brian is of uncertain origin. It may be Celtic in origin and it has long been popular in Ireland, because of the famous King Brian Boroimhe (941-1014). The name was known in Scotland during the reign of William the Lion (1165-1214), having come to Scotland from England, possibly having originated in Brittany. It was popular in Scotland around the middle of the twentieth century, but it faded from fashion later in the century.

Bruce

Bruce is one of several common Scottish surnames that became first names. The surname is of Norman extraction, probably coming from a

Norman place name, and dates from the Norman Conquest. Various places in northern France have been suggested as its derivation. The surname is particularly popular because of Robert the Bruce who became King of Scots and defeated the English at the famous Battle of Bannockburn in 1314. The use of the name as a male first name is much more recent, not becoming popular until the twentieth century. The name became particularly popular in Australia.

Callum, Calum

Callum, with its variant Calum, is a Gaelic form of the name Columba which is derived from the Latin word for 'dove'. Columba was an Irish monk, but he became famous in Scottish history because he left his native Ireland in 563 to become a missionary in Scotland. He and his followers founded a monastery on the Hebridean island of Iona that became the centre of Celtic Christianity in Scotland. The names Callum and Calum have become more widespread in recent times as names of Celtic origin have become extremely popular. Callum appears in the top ten in recent lists of most popular boys' names in Scotland.

Cameron

Cameron, better known as a Scottish surname and ancient clan name, is also used as a first name. The most common explanation of its derivation is that it is a Gaelic name derived from the expression *cam shorn* meaning 'crooked nose'. However, it has been suggested that there was also a Lowland form of the name which was derived from a place name, perhaps also referring to something crooked, such as a crooked stream. The use of Cameron as a male first name is more recent than the surname. It has become so popular that it appears in the top ten in recent lists of most popular boys' names in Scotland. It has also begun to be used occasionally as a female first name, probably because of the influence of American celebrities of the name.

Campbell

Campbell, better known as a Scottish surname, came to be used as a male first name in Scotland in the 1930s. It is derived from the Gaelic expression *cam beul,* 'crooked mouth'.

Charles

Charles is derived from a Germanic word *ceorl*, meaning a 'man'. This became Carolus in Latin and Charles in France. The name was brought from France to England during the Norman Conquest. It was not especially popular in Scotland until it was taken up by the royal house of Stewart and then it became particularly popular with families who were Jacobite supporters. Those of the royal Stewarts who were called Charles were far from lucky. Charles I was beheaded, Charles II lived a long time in exile and Prince Charles Edward Stewart (Bonnie Prince Charlie) failed in his attempt to retrieve the throne for the Stewarts. Their misfortune, however, does not seem to have affected the popularity of the name Charles at that time. **Charlie** is a common pet form of Charles. Charlie is also used as a girl's name.

Christian

see **Christian** *in* **Girls' Names**

Christopher

The name Christopher is derived from Greek through the Latin Christopheros. The Greek name means 'bearer of Christ'. Although this is said to have been a reference to carrying Christ in the heart rather than physically, a legend arose that St Christopher, who became the patron saint of travellers, had carried Christ as a child across a river. The name became particularly popular in Scotland towards the end of the twentieth century.

Colin

In Scotland the name Colin is derived from the Gaelic word *cailean* meaning a 'youth'. The name was originally common in Gaelic-speaking areas and particularly popular among members of the clan Campbell. It then became very popular throughout Scotland until the end of the twentieth century when it rather faded from fashion. Colin is sometimes a short form of **Nicholas**.

Conall

Conall is a Celtic name meaning 'strong wolf'. This is the name of several characters in Irish legend, including the hero Conall Cernac, and has long been a popular male first name in Ireland. Recently it has become popular in Scotland with the increase in the use of Celtic names.

Conan

Conan is an Irish male first name meaning 'little hound'. It has been a common name in Ireland since early times and appears in early Irish legends. It came to Scotland from Ireland and has recently become popular with the increase in the use of Celtic names. Before its current popularity surge, the name was best known in Scotland because of its association with Sir Arthur Conan Doyle (1859-1930), creator of Sherlock Holmes.

Connor

Connor has become popular in Scotland with the recent increase in the popularity of Celtic names. Indeed, it appears in the top twenty in recent lists of most popular boys' names in Scotland.

Long before this it was popular in Ireland where it also had the forms **Conor** and **Connaire**. The name features in Irish mythology and is derived from Irish Gaelic *concobhar* meaning 'high desire'.

Craig

Craig was a originally a surname, later becoming a male first name. The Scots word *craig* means 'crag' or 'cliff', and it is found in various place names. The Gaelic form is *creag*.

Cuthbert

Cuthbert was the name of a seventh-century saint who was Bishop of Lindisfarne (685-7). The origin of the name is Old English, being made up of the elements *cuth* meaning 'famous' and *beorht*, meaning 'bright'. St Cuthbert was well-known in southern Scotland as well as northern England and his name became quite popular as both a male first name and later as a surname. Its popularity as a first name has not survived the test of time, possibly because during World War I it had to endure the ignominy of being a name given to someone who tried to evade military service.

Daniel

Daniel is Hebrew in origin and means 'God has judged'. The name has always enjoyed a certain degree of popularity because of its biblical connections. Daniel is a biblical prophet whose faith in God protected him in the lion's den and a book of the Bible is named after him. The name has become extremely popular in Scotland and appears in the top ten in recent lists of most popular boys' names. It has the diminutive forms **Dan** and **Danny**.

David

David, famous in the Bible as the unexpected slayer of the giant Goliath, is of Hebrew origin from a word meaning 'beloved'. The name has long been popular in Wales where St David, who flourished in the seventh century, is the patron saint, but it is also a long-term favourite in Scotland. The name first became popular there because of its royal connections. It was the name given to the youngest son of Malcolm Canmore and St Margaret who became king as David I in 1124. David was also the name given to a son of Robert the Bruce who became David

II in 1329. The name David has stood the test of time in Scotland. **Dave** is a widespread form of David, but **Davie** is a particularly Scottish short form. **Davina** (sometimes shortened to **Vina**) was once a common female form of David in Scotland.

Declan

The name Declan is derived from the name of an Irish saint, Deaglan. It has been popular in Ireland for some time and it has recently become popular in Scotland.

Donald

A Celtic name generally thought to mean 'world leader' or 'world rule', its modern Gaelic form being Domhnall. Donald is a very old name and is said to have been first recorded in a Roman inscription of 20 AD as the name of a British prince. The name was brought over from Ireland and became very popular in Scotland, particularly in the Highlands and Western Isles, so much so that, at one point, Donald was used as a common name for a Highlander. **Donnie** is a common short form of Donald in Scotland while **Don** has become a name in its own right.

Dougall, Dougal

Dougall, Dubhgall in Gaelic, means 'dark stranger' and was probably first used of the Danish Vikings who were darker than the Norwegian Vikings. Dougall, with the alternative spelling **Dougal**, became popular in the Highlands and then spread to the rest of Scotland. **Dougie** and **Doug** are popular short forms of the name Dougall and of the name **Douglas**.

Douglas

Douglas, derived from the Gaelic expression *dubh glas*, meaning 'black water' or 'black stream', was a popular surname before it became a male first name. It was used as a female first name at one point. Like **Dougall**, it is sometimes shortened to **Dougie** and **Doug**.

Drew

Drew, meaning 'sturdy', was introduced to England by the French at the time of the

Norman Conquest. However, in Scotland it is often a short form of **Andrew**.

Duncan

Duncan is derived from the Gaelic name Donnchadh, meaning 'brown warrior'. The name was brought to a worldwide audience by Shakespeare's tragedy *Macbeth* in which Macbeth murders King Duncan of Scotland and takes over his throne. Duncan was a real eleventh-century king, although much of Shakespeare's play is fiction, Duncan being killed in battle by Macbeth.

Dylan

Dylan is Welsh in origin and is the name of a legendary god of the sea. The name was popularized by the Welsh poet Dylan Thomas (1914-53). It has only recently become popular in Scotland, but it now appears in the top twenty in recent lists of most popular boys' names.

Edward

The name Edward is derived from two Old English words, *ead* meaning 'rich' and *weard* meaning 'guardian'. The name has enjoyed particular popularity in England and there have been several kings and other members of royal families who bore the name. One such English king was Edward I, known as Edward Longshanks, who was particularly disliked by the Scots because of his attempts to subjugate them. The name Edward has been known in Scotland since the thirteenth century and a brother of Robert the Bruce was called Edward, but it has not achieved the degree of popularity in Scotland that it has in England.

Elliot, Eliot, Eliott, Elliott

Elliot, with its alternative spellings, is of Greek and Hebrew origin, meaning 'The Lord is my God'.

Eric

The name Eric is Scandinavian in origin. There is some dispute over its derivation. One suggestion is that it was derived from the Old Norse words *einn* meaning 'one' and *rikr* meaning 'ruler', while another is that it is derived from Old Norse words meaning 'ever brave'. The name was brought to Britain by the Danes in the ninth century. It is not currently common in Scotland, but it achieved a degree of popularity in the early part of the twentieth century.

Esmé

see **Esmé, Esmée** *in* **Girls' Names**

Ethan

The name Ethan is Hebrew in origin and means 'constant' or 'steadfast'. It has recently become popular in Scotland.

Euan, Ewan

Euan and Ewan, which have long been popular in Scotland, especially in the Highlands, are Gaelic in origin, being forms of the Gaelic name Eoghann. In origin, the Gaelic name may be a form of the name **Eugene** meaning 'of noble birth'. In some parts of Scotland Eoghann was anglicized as **Hugh** because of perceived similarities in pronunciation. The form Euan is currently slightly more popular in Scotland. **Ewen** is another form of **Ewan**.
See **Hugh** *and* **Owen**.

Farquhar

Farquhar is a form of the Gaelic name Fearchar which means 'very dear one'. It was originally a male first name, particularly popular in the Highlands.

Fergus

Fergus is the anglicized form of the Gaelic Fearghas meaning 'supreme choice'. According to tradition, Fergus mac Erc, also known as Fergus Mor, was one of three brothers, the others being **Angus** and **Lorne**, who, around 503, came from Ireland to Scotland to settle in what became Dalriada. The short form is **Fergie**. *See* **Angus** *and* **Lorne**.

Finlay, Finley

Finlay is the anglicized from of the Gaelic name Fionnlagh which means 'fair hero'. Traditionally, it is the name of Macbeth's father who died around 1020. The name has been a male first name from early times, later becoming also a surname. The form **Finley** is also found. Less common as a first name variant is **Findlay**.

Forbes

Forbes is named after an Aberdeenshire place name, the name being derived from the Gaelic *forba-ais* meaning 'at the land or place'. Forbes was first a surname, later becoming a male first name. Although it is now pronounced as one syllable, the name was originally pronounced with two.

Francis

Francis is derived from the Latin *Franciscus*, meaning 'a Frenchman'. The name was popularized in much of Europe by St Francis of Assisi (1182-1226), who was originally named Giovanni. **Frank** is a diminutive form of the name, although this is now often found as a name in its own right. **Frances** is the feminine form of Francis.

Fraser, Frazer

Fraser, also spelt as **Frazer**, is derived from a Norman surname which had various forms such as de Friselle, de Friseliere and de Friesel. It is thought that the name may possibly have come from a place name in France, although such a place has not been identified. Fraser was a common surname in Scotland, especially in the Highlands, before becoming also a male first name.

Gavin

Gavin is the Scottish form of the name **Gawain** who was one of the most famous knights in stories about King Arthur, the French form of the name being **Gauvain**. The name is thought to be Celtic in origin, but its meaning is uncertain, although it has been linked with the Welsh word *gwalch* meaning 'hawk'. In the Arthurian legend Sir Gawain is the son of the King of Lothian and, according to one tradition, Sir Gawain himself was King of Galloway. It is, therefore, fitting that Gavin became such a popular name in Scotland. For a long time Gavin was essentially Scottish and it took a considerable time for the name to spread to other parts of the English-speaking world.

George

George, derived from the Greek Georgios meaning 'husbandman' or 'farmer', is particularly associated with England, St George being England's patron saint. The name came to Scotland in the fourteenth century, but has never been that common in Scotland. There is a particularly Scottish version of the name in the form of **Geordie**. **Dod** and **Doddie** are also possible Scottish short forms.

Gilbert

Gilbert is Germanic in origin, being derived from *gisil*, meaning 'pledge' or 'hostage', and *berth*, meaning 'bright' or 'famous'. The name was recorded in Scotland in the middle of the twelfth century.

Gilchrist

Gilchrist is a Scottish surname, but it was once a popular Scottish male first name. It is derived from the Gaelic *gille Criosd* meaning 'servant of Christ'. The word *gille* means 'youth' or 'servant' and it was often attached to the name of a saint to indicate that the youth was a devotee of the saint, as in *Gille Anndrais*, follower of St Andrew.

Giles

Giles is the name of a saint, the name being derived from the Greek word *aigidion*, a 'young goat'. St Giles became the patron saint of beggars and cripples. The name Giles came to England and Scotland from France during the Norman Conquest and came to be used both as a male and female first name. Giles is not a common name in Scotland today, but, when it is used, it is a masculine name. Several churches were dedicated to St Giles, the best known of these being the High Kirk in Edinburgh. The Latinized form of Giles is Egidius and the feminine form of this, Egidia, was sometimes used in Scotland instead of Giles. This may have been only the written form of the name which was originally pronounced as *Giles*. Giles as a female name probably eventually developed into **Julia**.

Gillean

Gillean is derived from the Gaelic *gille Eoin*, 'servant of St John'. It was used in the Highlands as a male first name, especially among members of the clan MacLean.

Gillies

Gillies is derived from *gille Losa*, 'servant of Jesus'. Originally, this was a male first name, used particularly in the Western Isles and in parts of the Highlands. It was occasionally used as a female first name and later became a surname.

Gordon

Gordon was a well-known Scottish surname and the name of an important clan long before it became a male first name. It is named after a place in Berwickshire, the name of this place being of uncertain origin. The name was quite slow to become a male first name but it gained popularity after 1885 when General Charles Gordon was killed near the end of the long siege of Khartoum and became a national hero in Britain.

Graeme, Graham

Graeme is the most popular modern spelling of this name when it is used as a male first name, although **Graham** is also found and **Grahame** is also occasionally used. The name was originally a surname with the spelling **Graham**. Although it is a name much associated with Scotland, Graham is actually English in origin, probably being derived from the town now called Grantham in Lincolnshire.

Grant

Grant was originally a surname and the name of a Scottish clan. The name is Norman in origin, *le grant* being a nickname for someone who was exceptionally tall and derived from the French *grand*, 'tall' or 'big'. The surname Grant is ancient, but as a male first name it is much more modern and may have come into being in North America rather than in Scotland.

Greg

Greg has become a popular male first name in Scotland and elsewhere. There are two possible origins of the name. It can be seen either as a short form of **Gregor** or as a derivative of the surname Greig or Greg.

Gregor

Gregor is the anglicized form of Gaelic Griogair and is obviously related to the name **Gregory** which was popularized in early times as a male first name by St Gregory (540-604), a pope known as Gregory the Great. Gregory later became the personal name of several other popes. The name is derived from a Greek word *gregorein* and a Latin word *gregorius* meaning 'watchful'.

Hamish

Hamish is an anglicized form of the Gaelic male first name **Seamus**, this being the Gaelic form of the popular name **James**. Hamish has never enjoyed much popularity outside Scotland and even in Scotland the name is not currently nearly as popular as it once was.

Harry

Harry was originally a pet form of **Henry**. It became a name in its own right, especially in Scotland, and has achieved greater popularity in Scotland than Henry. The name has been recorded in Scotland since the late sixteenth century.

Hector

Hector, meaning 'holding fast', is probably best known as the legendary Trojan hero who was killed by the Greek hero Achilles. The name came into use in Scotland from around the middle of the fourteenth century, becoming particularly popular in the western Highlands. It is thought that the popularity of the name in Scotland may be, at least in part, ascribed to the fact that the Gaelic name Eachann, meaning 'horseman', was anglicized as Hector, although the two names are unconnected.

Henry

Henry is Germanic in origin and is made up of the words *haim,* meaning 'home', and *ric,* meaning 'power' or 'ruler', giving Henry the meaning 'ruler or head of the household'. Perhaps because of this meaning the name was given to several kings, including eight kings of England. This English royal connection makes us associate the name particularly with England. However, the name is recorded in Scotland from the twelfth century, and it was quite popular for a long time, declining in popularity in the 1960s. *See* **Harry**.

Hugh

Hugh is Germanic in origin, meaning 'mind' or 'spirit'. The name was brought to England by the Normans and soon spread to Scotland. In some parts of Scotland, Hugh was used as an anglicization of Eoghann, a Gaelic name of which **Ewan** is the usual English form. This was because of perceived similarities in pronunciation between Hugh and Eoghann (*see* **Euan**, **Ewan**). Hugh was also used as an anglicization of **Aodh** (*see* **Aidan**).

Hunter

Hunter, derived from the occupation or activity of hunting, is a well-known Scottish surname. It is also occasionally used as a male first name.

Iain, Ian

Iain is a Gaelic form of **John**, long popular in Scotland. The name is often spelt Ian, especially outside Scotland. The spelling **Eoin** is now rare. *See* **John**.

Innes

see **Innes** *in* **Girls' Names**

Irvine, Irving

Irvine, more commonly a Scottish surname, is also sometimes used as a male first name. It is derived from a place name in Ayrshire. The name **Irving** is an alternative form in both first name and surname.

Ivor

Ivor was formerly quite commonly used as a male first name in those parts of Scotland which were subject to a marked Norse influence. The name comes from the Norse name **Ivarr** which is derived from words meaning 'yew' and 'warrior'.

Jack

Jack has long been a popular form of **John**, although it was probably a variant of the name Jacques, the French form of **James**. The name Jack was recorded in Scotland around the middle of the fifteenth century and was recorded as a surname only slightly later. Jack is now used as a name in its own right and appears in recent lists of the top ten most popular boys' names in Scotland.

See **John**.

Jamie

Once considered to be a form of **James**, Jamie is now used as a name in its own right. It has become particularly popular recently. It is now also used as a female name.

See **James**.

James

James, the Latin form of which is Jacobus, is a common male first name in English-speaking countries. This may well have been originally because of the name's biblical connections since two of the apostles of Jesus were called James. The name James has enjoyed particular popularity in Scotland because of its royal connections, there having been seven King James of Scotland, not to mention James, the Old Pretender, whom the Jacobites wanted to make James VIII. It is still fashionable, appearing in the top ten in recent lists of most popular boys' names. Short

or informal forms of the name include **Jim**, **Jimmy**, and **Jamie**. In the Glasgow area Jimmy is used as an informal form of address to a male who is not known to the speaker.
See **Hamish**.

Jay

Jay is often used as a nickname for people beginning with the letter 'J', as in **James**, **John** etc. Jay is now often used as a name in its own right and has several possible derivations. It can be derived from the bird of the name, from the Latin name Gaius, meaning 'happy', or from a Sanskrit word meaning 'victory'.

Jimmy

see **James**

Jock

Jock is a common Scottish form of the name **John**, being the equivalent of the English name Jack. It sometimes takes the form **Jockie**. Jock is often used as a term for a Scottish soldier, particularly a Highlander, and is sometimes used by non-Scots to refer to a Scotsman, just as Taffy is used for a Welshman. *See* **John**.

John

John has long been a very popular male first name in Scotland, even more so than in the rest of the English-speaking countries where it has also enjoyed great popularity. Hebrew in origin, the name means 'God has been gracious' and it goes back to biblical times; John the Baptist being the son of Elizabeth, sister of the Virgin Mary. *See* **Jack**, **Jock** and **Ian**.

Jonathan

Jonathan is Hebrew in origin meaning 'Jehovah has given'. In the Bible the most famous Jonathan is the son of Saul who was a close friend of David. The name was recorded in Scotland at the end of the twelfth century, but was not at all popular in Scotland until the second part of the twentieth century and has now faded again from fashion.

Joseph

Joseph is Hebrew in origin meaning 'Jehovah will add', indicating that God will add other children to the one already born. There are several Josephs in the Bible, principally the Old Testament Joseph who was the son of Jacob and Rachel and who is known for his 'coat of many colours', and the New Testament Joseph who was the husband of the Virgin Mary. The name has been in use since the Middle Ages and was popular in Scotland until it faded from fashion in the second part of the twentieth century. Recently the name has experienced a resurgence of popularity in Scotland. **Joe** is a common short form and **Josephine** is the feminine form.

Josh, Joshua

In the Old Testament in the Bible Joshua is the name of the Israelite leader who took the children of Israel into the Promised Land after the death of Moses. The name is Hebrew in origin, meaning 'Jehovah is salvation'. The name came to Scotland after the Reformation, but it is only recently that it has become popular, and the short form **Josh**, now a name in its own right, is considerably more popular than the longer name.

Keith

As a name, Keith was originally a Scottish surname which became particularly common in the north-east of the country. Later it became a male first name and spread to other parts of the English-speaking world. Before that it was a Scottish place name and it was probably derived from a word meaning 'wood'.

Kenneth

Kenneth is associated with two Gaelic names Cinead, meaning 'born of fire' and Coinneach meaning 'handsome one'. St Cainnech, an Irish abbot, visited St Columba on Iona and Kenneth MacAlpin, often regarded as the first King of Scotland, may have been called after him. Certainly Kenneth MacAlpin would have popularized the male first name Kenneth in Scotland. Kenneth is sometimes shortened to either **Ken** or **Kenny**.

Kevin

Kevin is an Irish name which became popular in Scotland in the second part of the twentieth century, although it has now faded from fashion. There is some dispute about its origin, but it is generally thought to be derived from the Irish Gaelic Caoimhin, meaning 'born comely'.

Kieran

Kieran is an anglicization of the Irish Celtic name **Ciaran**, pronounced *keer-an,* meaning 'little dark one', from the adjective *ciar*, 'dark'. Ciaran, the name of several Irish saints, has long been popular in Ireland and Kieran has become popular in Scotland with the increase in interest in Celtic names. **Kiera** and **Keira** are feminine forms.

Kyle

Kyle was originally a surname, named after a district of Ayrshire, which was, in turn, named after Coel, ruler of the district around 400 AD, perhaps the King Cole of nursery rhyme fame. The surname Kyle was first recorded in the fifteenth century. It is currently enjoying much popularity as a first name. Its popularity may, in part, be due to the fact that it sounds Irish and Celtic names have become extremely popular throughout Britain. There is a feminine form **Kyla**. The girl's name **Kylie**, popularized by the Australian singer Kylie Minogue, may also have connections with it.

Lachlan

Lachlan is a Scottish male first name, the Gaelic spelling of which is Lachlann or Lachann. The name may be derived from a Norse word for 'lakeland' or 'fjordland'. It has been suggested that Lachlan may have originally been used of an immigrant to Scotland from Norway, land of the fjords. Another suggestion is that Lachlan is Irish in origin, being derived from *lough-lann* meaning 'lake habitation'. Lachlan is often shortened to **Lachie**.

Leslie

As a name, Leslie was originally a Scottish surname, derived from a place name in Aberdeenshire, originally called Lesslyn. Leslie then became a male first name and later the feminine form **Lesley** came into being. The distinction between the use of Leslie for men and Lesley for women has become blurred over the years.

Lewis

You would be forgiven for thinking that the name Lewis has been derived from the Hebridean island of the name and doubtless some parents have named their sons Lewis because of a connection with the island. However, the name Lewis is not of Scottish origin. Instead, it comes from a Germanic word meaning 'famous warrior' which was Latinized as Ludovicus. In French this became **Louis** and the name was given to several French kings. The name was brought to England by the Normans, taking the spelling **Lewis**, and it gradually made its way to Scotland. The name has steadily become more and more popular in Scotland and is now in the top ten in recent lists of most popular boys' names in Scotland.

Liam

Liam is a diminutive form of **Uilliam**, the Irish form of **William** which was taken to Ireland by twelfth-century Norman invaders. Celtic names, both Scottish and Irish, have recently become very popular in Scotland. Liam is particularly liked, appearing in the top ten in recent lists of the most popular boys' names in Scotland. *See* **William**.

Lindsay

see **Lindsay** *in* **Girls' Names**

Logan

Logan was originally a Scottish surname, being derived from a Gaelic word meaning 'little hollow'. It then became a male first name, at first quite rare, but recently very popular. Indeed, Logan appears in the top ten in recent lists of most popular boys' names in Scotland.

Lorne

Lorne is a Scottish male first name. It has never been common, although it is a name of great antiquity. According to tradition, Lorne was the name of one of three brothers, the others being **Angus** and **Fergus**, who, around 503, came from Ireland to Scotland to settle in what became Dalriada. *See* **Angus** *and* **Fergus**.

Louis

see **Lewis**

Luke

Luke is derived from the Greek Loukas, meaning 'man from Lucania', a region of southern Italy. In the Bible Luke was an apostle and physician. When the name first came to Britain it took the form **Lucas**, but the shorter form Luke soon became more popular.

Magnus

Magnus is a Latin word meaning 'great'. The name of the ultra-powerful eighth-century emperor Charlemagne was simply an adaptation of the Latin form of his name, Carolus Magnus. The Norwegians and Danes made the Magnus part of this a male first name and took it with them when they travelled to Scotland and occupied parts of it. The name Magnus became particularly popular in the Orkneys and Shetland. The Gaelic form of the name in Ireland and Scotland is Manus.

Malcolm

Malcolm is derived from the Gaelic *Maol Coluim* meaning 'servant or devotee of St Columba'. The name has long been popular in Scotland, perhaps originally because of its royal associations. Four kings of Scotland were called Malcolm, the most famous of them being Malcom III, known as Malcolm Canmore (1031-93), husband of St Margaret.

Mark

Mark is the equivalent of the Latin name Marcus which is derived from Mars, the Roman god of war. It is the name of one of the apostles in the Bible. Mark was not commonly used in Scotland until after the Reformation, later becoming widely used around the middle of the twentieth century. It became even more popular from the 1970s, but has faded from popularity recently in Scotland. **Marcus** also exists as a male first name.

Martin

Martin has linguistic associations with Mars, the Roman god of war. Perhaps because of Martin of Tours, a fourth-century saint who aroused much devotion and admiration, Martin became a popular male first name throughout Europe, including Scotland, in the early centuries. However, its popularity as a first name in Scotland was overtaken by its popularity as a surname.

Matthew

Matthew is a name of Hebrew origin meaning 'gift of God'. Matthew has biblical associations, being the name of one of the twelve apostles of Jesus. The name was common in Scotland in the Middle Ages and only really faded from popularity in the early twentieth century. Recently, with a renewed interest in old names, including biblical names, Matthew has regained its popularity in Scotland.

Michael

Michael is derived from Hebrew and means 'who is like God'. The name of one of the archangels in the Bible, Michael became a popular first name in the Middle Ages in Christian countries and it has retained its popularity in Scotland. The name has been known in Scotland since the thirteenth century and later gave rise to the surname **Mitchell**, possibly as a result of French influence. Short forms include **Mike** and **Mick**. Michael has the feminine forms **Michelle**, which came from France, and **Michaela**.

Mungo

Mungo, thought to mean 'dear one', was a kind of nickname given to St Kentigern, the patron saint of the city of Glasgow and Bishop of Cumbria. It is possible that the name was later popularized by the well-known eighteenth-century Scottish explorer Mungo Park (1771-1806).

Murdo

Murdo is Celtic in origin, having linguistic connections with the Gaelic word *muir* meaning 'the sea'. It is probably derived from the Gaelic name Murchadh meaning 'sea warrior'.

Murray

Murray, sometimes spelt **Moray**, is of Gaelic origin and means 'lord and master'.

Nathan

Nathan is Hebrew in origin, meaning 'God has given'. It is the name of a prophet at the court of King David in the Old Testament in the Bible. The name is recorded in Scotland in the late seventeenth century, but only recently became popular.

Neil, Niall

Neil is a common Scottish male first name, derived from Irish **Niall**, meaning 'champion'. Niall was popular in Ireland from early times because of the fame of the semi-legendary Niall of the Nine Hostages. The spelling Niall has now become quite popular in Scotland with the recent increase in interest in Celtic names. **Nigel** is a form of Neil, perhaps because the letter *g* was wrongly inserted when the name was transcribed into Latin, although the name Nigel has never been particularly associated with Scotland.

Nicholas

Nicholas is Greek in origin from *nike*, meaning 'victory' and *laos*, meaning 'people'. The name was popularized by St Nicholas who was the patron saint of children, among others, and became known as Santa Claus. Nicholas was known in Scotland by the twelfth century. **Nick** is a common diminutive form and is now a name in its own right. **Nicole** and **Nicola** are feminine forms.

Nigel

see **Neil**, **Niall**

Ninian

Ninian is a Scottish male first name, once also common in Northumberland and Yorkshire. The name originated in Scotland with the fourth-century St Ninian who converted some of the Picts and Britons to Christianity.

Norman

Norman is Germanic in origin and means 'north man'. The name was used in England before the

Norman Conquest in 1066. In Scotland it became particularly associated with the clan McLeod and then became generally quite common until it fell out of fashion from the second part of the twentieth century. **Norrie** is a diminutive form of the name.

Oliver

The name is traditionally associated with the olive and may be derived from the old French name Olivier. However, it has been suggested that the name may be a form of a Germanic name which also gave rise to the Scandinavian name Olaf. The name was known in Scotland in the late twelfth century and it was fairly common until the middle of the seventeenth century when its associations with Oliver Cromwell drove it out of fashion. It became quite popular again in Scotland in the nineteenth century. **Ollie** and **Noll** are diminutive forms.

Owen

Owen is said to be a Welsh form of the Latin name Eugenius, Eugene, meaning 'well-born'. It is particularly associated with Wales, but it has also long been popular in Ireland where it was originally Eoghan. The name Eoghan was taken to Scotland by the Irish when the country was known as Dalriada, and it later became Owen. *See* **Euan**, **Ewan**.

Patrick

Patrick, derived from the Latin word *patricius,* meaning a 'patrician' or 'nobleman', is a name much associated with Ireland and the Irish and it is the name of their patron saint. However, it was established in Scotland fairly early on and was in relatively common use among some families at least in the fifteenth century. It enjoyed a renewal of popularity when a great many Irish families emigrated to Scotland in the mid-nineteenth century after the failure of the potato harvest. **Pat** is a common diminutive of the name, also being used for the feminine form **Patricia**. **Paddy** is a less common diminutive form and is sometimes used to refer to an Irishman in the way that Jock is used to refer to a Scotsman. **Padruig**, **Paruig** and **Padair** or **Patair** are Gaelic forms of the name **Peter**. Because of this last Gaelic form of the

name, some confusion arose between this and
the name Peter.

Paul

Paul is derived from the Latin *paulis,* meaning
'small'. It was popularized by the biblical St
Paul who changed his name from Saul when
he became a Christian. The name was known
in Scotland in the twelfth century and became
more common after the Reformation. Paul
became particularly popular in Scotland in the
second part of the twentieth century, but it has
faded from popularity now. **Pauline** and **Paula**
are feminine forms of Paul.

Peter

Peter, together with its various forms in other
countries, was very popular for a long time
in most of the Christian world because of its
biblical connections. It was the name given by
Jesus to Simon, a Galilean fisherman who became
the most important apostle. Peter means a 'rock',
being derived from the Greek word *petros*. It
has been as popular in Scotland as elsewhere,
but its popularity faded towards the end of the

twentieth century. **Pete** is a common diminutive form of Peter.

Philip

The name Philip is derived from the Greek words *philein*, 'to love', and *hippos*, 'a horse', giving 'love of horses'. The name was known in Scotland in the twelfth century, but it has never been particularly popular in Scotland, certainly not as popular as it has been in England and Wales. **Philippa** is the feminine form and **Phil** a common diminutive form.

Richard

Richard is Germanic in origin meaning 'hardy ruler' or 'brave ruler'. It has no special connections with Scotland, although the name is generally popular in the English-speaking world and Scotland is no exception. The Normans brought the name to England and it had spread to Scotland by the twelfth century. The name was more popular in England, partly because of its royal connections, starting with Richard I (1157-99), Richard the Lion Heart, who was famous for his part in the Crusades. Richard has the common short forms **Dick**, **Dickie**, **Rick**, **Richie** and **Ritchie**.

Reece, Rhys

Rhys is a Welsh name, derived from *ris*, meaning 'ardour' or 'enthusiasm', which has become popular in Scotland. Rhys is pronounced *rees* and the spelling **Reece** is slightly more common than Rhys in Scotland.

Robbie

Robbie was originally a diminutive form of **Robert**. Now it is a name in its own right in Scotland.

Robert

Robert has enjoyed great popularity in Scotland as a male first name, although the name is not Scottish by derivation. Instead, it is Germanic in origin, being derived from two words: *hrothi* meaning 'fame' and *bertha* meaning 'bright'. An early famous bearer of the name was Robert the Bruce who became King of Scots as Robert I (1274-1329) and is remembered for his victory against the English at the Battle of Bannockburn in 1314. Robert has several diminutive forms, such as **Rob** and **Robbie** and **Bob** and **Bobbie**. These diminutives are not restricted to Scotland but the diminutive forms **Rab** and **Rabbie** tend to be so. **Robin** was sometimes used as a form of Robert in Scotland.

Robin

see **Robert**, *also* **Robin**, **Robyn** *in* **Girls' Names**

Roderick

Roderick is an anglicized form of the Gaelic name **Ruaridh** which means 'red king'. The name Roderick was common among certain Scottish clans and more generally quite common in Scotland in the nineteenth century. Roderick has the diminutive forms **Roddie** and **Rod**. Ruaridh has more commonly been anglicized as **Rory**.

Roger

Roger is Germanic in origin, the Old English equivalent being Hrothgar, derived from *hroth* meaning 'fame' and *ger*, a 'spear'. The name was introduced to England by the Normans and spread to Scotland by the twelfth century, although it has never become particularly popular.

Ronan

Ronan comes from the Irish word *ron* which means 'seal'. The name has recently become quite popular in Scotland as well as in Ireland, with the recent increase in the use of Celtic names.

Rory

Rory is an anglicized form of the Gaelic name **Ruaridh** meaning 'red king'. The name is enjoying current popularity with the increase in interest in Celtic names, as, indeed, is Ruaridh itself. Ruaridh has also been anglicized as **Roderick**.

Ross

Ross was a common Scottish surname long before it became a male first name. The surname Ross is derived from the Scottish place name meaning 'promontory' or 'woodland'. It probably came into use as a first name in the nineteenth century in Scotland.

Rowan

Rowan was originally used both as a male first name and a female one in Scotland. More recently, the female name has become more common.
See **Rowan** *in* **Girls' Names**.

Roy

Roy is a male first name derived from the Gaelic word *ruad* meaning 'red'. The name was originally a nickname for someone with red hair. Stories and legends about the Scottish outlaw Rob Roy McGregor (1671-1734), often known just as Rob Roy, helped to popularize the name Roy.

Ruaridh

see **Roderick** *and* **Rory**

Ryan

The name Ryan is a common Irish surname which became a male first name. Following the recent increase in the use of Celtic names, both